Dorothea Lange

Photographer of the People

Dorothea Lange

Photographer of the People

David C. King

Sharpe Focus
an imprint of M.E. Sharpe, Inc.

SERIES CONSULTANT

Jeffrey W. Allison
Paul Mellon Collection
Educator, Virginia Museum of Fine Arts

Cover Art:
"Migrant Mother" (Dorothea Lange);
"San Francisco Social Security Office" (Dorothea Lange).

Sharpe Focus
An imprint of M.E. Sharpe, Inc.
80 Business Park Drive
Armonk, NY 10504
www.sharpe-focus.com

Series created by Kid Graphica, LLC
Series designed by Gilda Hannah
Map: Mapping Specialists Limited

Library of Congress Cataloging-in-Publication Data

King, David C.
Dorothea Lange: photographer of the people / by David C. King.
    p. cm. — (Show me America)
Includes bibliographical references and index.
ISBN 978-0-7656-8154-6 (hardcover: alk. paper)
1. Lange, Dorothea—Juvenile literature. 2. Women photographers—United States—
Biography—Juvenile literature. 3. Photographers—United States—Biography—
Juvenile literature. I. Title.

TR140.L3K45 2008
770.92—dc22
[B]   2007040696

Printed in Malaysia

9 8 7 6 5 4 3 2 1

Contents

In Her Own Words

The camera is an instrument that teaches people how to see without a camera.

One should really use the camera as though tomorrow you'd be stricken blind.

To live a visual life is an enormous undertaking, practically unattainable. I've only touched it, just touched it.

Artists are controlled by the life that beats in them, like the ocean beats on the shore.

You force yourself onto strange streets, among strangers. It may be very hot. It may be painfully cold. It may be sandy and windy and you say, "What am I doing here? What drives me to do this hard thing?"

I very early remember that my grandmother told me that of all the things that were beautiful in the world there was nothing finer than an orange, as a thing . . . and I knew what she meant, perfectly.

I have learned from everything, and I'm constantly learning. It's part curiosity, I think, trying to discover why things happen the way they do, watching everything, my own activities included.

Lange holds her camera on her favorite perch for taking pictures.

CHAPTER ONE

A Photographer's First Observations

I invented my own photographic schooling as
I went along, stumbling into most of it.
–Dorothea Lange

Dorothea Margarette Nutzhorn was born in 1895 in Hoboken, New Jersey, to a well-to-do German American family. The first few years of her life were comfortable and happy. Her father, Henry Nutzhorn, was a successful lawyer. They lived in a substantial brownstone house. Hoboken was a small, quiet port town across the Hudson River from New York City.

Two events shattered the normality of her childhood, and both left painful scars that would shape her life. In 1902, when she was seven (a year after her brother, Martin, was born), Dorothea was stricken with polio, also known as infantile paralysis. It was a frightening and painful disease, with no known cause or cure. For days, her young body was wracked with fever and pain.

Dorothea survived the illness, but her right leg was permanently damaged, leaving her with a severe limp that could never be corrected. The limp made her painfully self-conscious, especially when neighborhood children teased her and called her "Limpy." Her mother made things worse by loudly telling her to walk straighter when they met people on the street.

"I think it perhaps was the most important thing that happened to me," Dorothea later recalled. "It formed me, guided me, instructed me, helped me, and humiliated me. All those things at once. I've never gotten over it, and I am aware of the force and the power of it."

Dorothea and her mother rode the ferry every day from the Hoboken Ferry Port across the Hudson River to Manhattan.

Five years later, when Dorothea was twelve, the second devastating event occurred when her father abandoned the family without a word. He left no address or money, and they never heard from him again. The family was left penniless and had to move in with Dorothea's grandmother, Sophie Lange, a skilled dressmaker. In response to the pain of her father's abandonment, Dorothea dropped his name, Nutzhorn, and took her grandmother's name of Lange.

To support the family, Dorothea's mother, Joan, got a job at the New York Public Library. She enrolled Dorothea in a New York City school, and, each morning, she and her daughter took the ferry from Hoboken to Manhattan.

Opposite: Dorothea loved the bustling, noisy streets of Manhattan's Lower East Side. "I would get so far on the way to school," she said, "and then I'd turn and walk the streets."

Dorothea was uneasy around the homeless men
on the Bowery, but that did not keep her away.

Often bored by school, Dorothea was not a very good student. She was much more interested in the crowded, noisy streets of Manhattan's Lower East Side, where thousands of new immigrants filled the air with a cacophony of shouts, threats, laughter, songs, vendors' calls, cries, and arguments. The years from 1890 to 1910 brought millions of hopeful newcomers from Eastern and Southern Europe—Poles, Russians, Greeks, Italians, and more. Most of these immigrants entered the United States at Ellis Island, a short distance from the inspiring Statue of Liberty.

After school, and on the countless days that she skipped school, Dorothea roamed the bustling streets. She found beauty and human interest even in the midst of the poverty and squalor. She was careful, and very frightened, when she had to thread her way among the drunken homeless men on the Bowery, a large, busy street on the Lower East Side of Manhattan. In later years, she wrote, "I realize how enriched I am through having been on the loose in my formative years. I have known all my life so many people who have always done what they should do, been proper, made the grades—and lost."

Dorothea managed to complete just enough work in high school to graduate in 1914. Her mother, worried about her daughter's future, asked what she planned to do. "I want to be a photographer," Dorothea answered simply, even though she did not own a camera and had never taken a photograph. But her years of observing the details of life in New York had made her eager to capture what she saw in photographs. Her mother, however, was insistent that Dorothea study to be a teacher, one of the few careers open to women in the early 1900s. An unwilling Dorothea enrolled in the New York Training School for Teachers.

Dorothea remained determined to become a photographer, however. There were no schools of photography in those years, so she designed her own apprenticeship program. "I invented my own photographic schooling as I went along," she recalled, "stumbling into most of it."

Dorothea boldly went to the studio of Arnold Genthe, one of New York's most famous portrait photographers. Although she had no experience, Genthe must have been impressed by her eagerness and intelligence. He hired her at a salary of $15 a week—a decent wage for part-time work in those days—and trained her in setting up the lights and operating the big, cumbersome camera.

Genthe also introduced Dorothea to some of New York's wealthiest and most famous people. She learned to make these people feel comfortable during long sittings in front of the camera, and watched with fascination as Genthe worked his camera magic from all possible angles. Observing Genthe provided an important element in Lange's approach to photography. Author Susannah Abbey stated it this way:

> [Genthe] didn't just snap their picture; he seemed to make the camera understand the people. This sense that an understanding of a subject was essential in making a portrait was truly the artistic part of photography, and something that Dorothea would take with her for the rest of her career.

After two years, Dorothea left Genthe's studio and worked briefly with several other photographers. Each job taught her something new, and she also took one of the few photography courses available. The course, at Columbia University, was taught by another famous photographer—Clarence White. Although White did not communicate easily with his students, he helped Dorothea develop increasing confidence in her own ability.

Meanwhile, her teacher-training program was not going well. She disliked the stuffy classrooms and the endless lectures. Then, when she had to practice-teach a fifth-grade class, everything fell apart. The children quickly discovered that Dorothea did not know how to control them, so they began climbing out the window and

Arnold Genthe was one of New York's most famous
portrait photographers and Dorothea's first teacher.

THE ART OF THE DARKROOM

Dorothea was convinced that in order to become a professional photographer she had to learn how to develop her own photographs. The technique proved more difficult than she had imagined, but with the help of the traveling photographer, she gradually mastered the fundamentals.

The first step was to cover the windows with thick black paper to make the room completely dark. A dim yellow lamp, called a safelight, provided enough light for her to remove the negatives from the camera and soak them in trays of "chemical baths." Gradually, the image emerged. The image was in reverse, with black where white would be and vice versa.

Dorothea hung the negatives on a string until they were dry. She then placed each dry negative against a sheet of photographic paper and exposed it briefly to a bright light before placing the paper in a bath of developer. She rocked the tray gently, letting the developer wash over the emerging positive image on the paper. When she was satisfied that the contrast between black and white was right, she took the paper out of the bath, rinsed it, and hung it up to dry. The photograph was finished.

down the fire escape to the playground. Her supervisor easily restored order, as Dorothea watched with tears of humiliation streaming down her face.

After this incident, even her mother was convinced that Dorothea was not cut out for teaching, and she did not object when her daughter withdrew from the program. Dorothea bought a view camera with an accordian-pleated bellows and two lenses.

While she practiced taking photos of neighborhood children, a traveling photographer helped her transform the family's chicken coop into a darkroom that they both could use. He also taught her how to develop her own pictures.

Having learned the basics of darkroom work, Dorothea decided the time had come to leave Hoboken and strike out on her own. Throughout her childhood and adolescence, she had made only one close friend, Florence Ahlstrom, usually known by her nickname of Fronzie.

In January 1918, the two young women set out on what was to be their great adventure—a trip around the world. They got as far as San Francisco.

In 1918, when Dorothea Lange arrived in San Francisco, her new home had recovered from the devastating 1906 earthquake and fire.

CHAPTER TWO

In Love with San Francisco

> I seriously tried, with every person [I photographed],
> to reveal them as closely as I could.
> —*Dorothea Lange*

Dorothea Lange and her friend Fronzie Ahlstrom reached San Francisco with about $140 in cash between them. It's hard to imagine how they planned to travel around the world with such a small sum, but they were adventurous, and Lange thought she could take photographic portraits of wealthy people on the ship.

They didn't have to wonder about travel funds for long, however. On their first night in San Francisco, a thief stole Ahlstrom's wallet, which held all their money.

The two young women recovered quickly. Within twenty-four hours, they had checked into the Episcopal Home for Working Girls, and both had found jobs. Ahlstrom started work with Western Union, sending telegrams, and Lange was hired to develop photos in a department store.

Lange quickly fell in love with San Francisco. The city had been a magnet for people seeking fortune and adventure since the Gold Rush days of the 1840s and 1850s. The devastating earthquake and fire of 1906 had destroyed much of the city, but by 1918, when Lange and Ahlstrom arrived, the city was booming again.

San Francisco drew a great variety of people. Chinese, Italians, and Mexicans formed their own distinctive neighborhoods. Business people, bankers, construction workers, and professionals such as doctors, lawyers, and architects came in search of opportunity. Ranchers, cowboys, farmhands, seamen, and gamblers thronged to the city looking for a good time.

Imogen Cunningham's photograph of Dorothea Lange.

Aside from New York, no other city could boast such a large population of artistic people. Painters, writers, poets, musicians, actors, and dancers formed a colorful subculture and were known as "Bohemians." Lange said that Bohemians were "the free and easy livers. They were people who lived according to their own standards and did what they wanted to do in the way they wanted to do it." Some of them belonged to the San Francisco Camera Club, of which Lange became a member.

Dorothea Lange's portrait of Imogen Cunningham.

The Bohemian Life

Life in San Francisco brought dramatic changes to Lange, and those changes began when the Bohemians welcomed her into their circle. On her first day of work developing photographs, she met an artist named Roi Partridge and his wife, Imogen Cunningham, a well-known photographer. They introduced her to their Bohemian group and became her friends for life.

THE GREAT GRAFLEX CAMERA

The Graflex camera was first manufactured in 1902 and, with improvements, remained the standard for professional photographers from the 1920s to the 1950s. The Speed Graphic was the best model of this folding camera. It was remarkably rugged and could even be repaired in the field.

The camera, which is now a collectors' item, was a handsome wooden box, covered with leather. With the viewfinder on the side and a complex series of steps to follow before shooting, the Graflex was not easy to use. But it took first-rate photos, with sharp detail and excellent depth of field (focusing clearly on details both close and farther away). The Rolleiflex, a competing camera, was simpler to use, but the quality of the photos it took was not as good. The Folmer and Schwing Company ended production of the Graflex camera in 1973.

A sturdy Graflex camera. A camera, Lange said, "is an instrument that teaches us to see without a camera."

Through her new friends, Lange met two wealthy men who provided the financial backing for her to open her own portrait studio. It was a remarkable stroke of luck. In 1919, barely six months after her arrival in the city, she opened a studio on Sutter Street and began taking photographs of some of San Francisco's wealthiest and most influential people. She worked in the studio until 1925.

While her studio became an instant success, another important change in Lange's life came about because she was so unhappy about her disability—the withered leg and severe limp left by her bout with polio. Some of her attempts to cope with her misery were not successful and only made her feel worse. She tried to force herself to walk straighter, for example, and even took ballroom dancing to improve her stride.

Gradually, Lange found that she could partially disguise the limp by the way she dressed. She began wearing long, swirling skirts. To add to her Bohemian style, she wore large, heavy silver necklaces and bracelets, plus a black beret, which she cocked to one side in the style of a French artist.

Her new style gave her self-confidence and helped make her studio one of the important gathering places for Bohemians. She hired a young Chinese American woman as a combination photographic assistant and maid. Every afternoon, the assistant served tea to the ever-changing gathering of Bohemians who collected at "Dorie's," as she was often called.

Dorothea Lange set up each portrait to bring out the character of the subject. This is her childhood friend, Fronzie Ahlstrom.

Lange applied what she had learned in New York studios to her new business of taking photographic portraits. One of her first clients was a well-to-do San Francisco woman who was so impressed by Lange's work that she urged her friends to patronize the new studio.

Lange spent a lot of time with each subject, getting to know the person so that she could draw out key features of the sitter's personality. She used a large camera on a tripod; it made negatives on 8- by 10-inch (20- by 25-centimeter) glass plates. "I seriously tried, with every person," she said, "to reveal them as closely as I could." The clients, in turn, were convinced that Lange was capturing their true character.

In addition, visits to the Sutter Street studio were something of an adventure for her clients. Her long skirts, exotic jewelry, and unusual way of walking due to her limp made her seem a perfect representative of the artistic, free-spirited Bohemians. She soon had enough work to keep her busy for long hours every day, as well as most weekends.

Lange's photographic style and her personality made her a perfect chronicler of one of the most unusual and exciting decades in the country's history. The "Roaring Twenties" was a remarkable time, when life seemed to move at a faster pace than ever before. New inventions, such as automobiles, airplanes, radios, motion pictures, and a host of electric appliances and gadgets gave middle-class and wealthy Americans new ways to enjoy life. The nation's experiment with Prohibition, which made alcohol illegal, led people to drink in underground bars, called "speakeasies." New forms of music, especially jazz, and new dance steps also contributed to the flashy lifestyle of those who could afford it. In addition, "playing" the stock market led to a few quick fortunes and the illusion that anyone in America could get rich overnight.

While Lange gained modest fame by making a portrait record of the decade's rich and famous, her life and career soon led her in important new directions.

Balancing Family and Work

Through her friends Partridge and Cunningham, Lange met a well-known artist named Maynard Dixon, twenty years her senior. Tall, thin, and handsome, Dixon had spent many years in the Southwest painting large canvases of the people, the wildlife, and the scenery, from mountains to deserts. Lange was captivated by him. Observing him surrounded by her studio guests, she wrote that "he was the kind legends cluster about, without his making any particular effort. I have never watched any person's life as closely as I watched his, what it held, how he lived it."

Lange's photograph of a Navajo Indian boy
shows her new determination to photograph *all*
Americans, regardless of class, race, or ethnicity.

Maynard Dixon with their sons, Dan and John. Juggling home and work would be a lifelong struggle for Lange.

Within six months of their meeting, Dorothea and Maynard were married on March 21, 1920. She was twenty-four and he was forty-five. Fronzie Ahlstrom was her maid of honor, and Roi Partridge was his best man.

Marriage immediately complicated Dorothea Lange's life. For the next fifteen years, she was torn between the demands of her work and her marriage. In the 1920s, it was still unusual for a married woman to work outside the home, especially when children were involved. Lange took this double responsibility seriously, particularly when she tried for a time having Dixon's ten-year-old daughter live with them. Lange rushed home from her studio to prepare dinner; there were no more afternoon teas accompanied by discussion, music, and dancing.

Even after her stepdaughter went to live with friends, Lange's conflict remained, deepening with the birth of her two sons: John, born May 15, 1925, and Daniel, June 12, 1928. Raising the boys and trying to keep her photography career active was not the only source of conflict.

Dixon was deeply committed to his art. He was away from home for long stretches, often up to four months. Lange seemed to accept this. In an interview with a newspaper reporter, she was asked how she managed marriage to an artist. "It's simple," she said. "Simple that is, when an artist's wife accepts the fact that he needs a certain amount of freedom—freedom from the petty, personal things of life."

The fifteen years of their marriage were a rocky time for Lange. She tried to provide everything her husband needed, but she rarely had time for her own work. Some of their best moments were when the whole family spent time in the Southwest. Lange did not have much time to work, but when she did, she began to take pictures outside of the makeshift studio she had set up.

Without being aware of it, her camera work began to undergo a major change to a more documentary style. Viewers of her work, she recalled later, "were able to sense, if not see, a good deal more about the subject than just faces. They were *larger* photographs." She also began to take pictures of Native Americans, Mexicans, and other local people. Such subjects were unusual in the 1920s, but Dixon helped her understand that it was important for the public to see *all* the faces of America.

In the early 1930s, Dorothea Lange's life and career changed dramatically again, when the nation faced one of its greatest challenges—the Great Depression.

This photo, called "White Angel Bread Line," of
a man alone with his despair became one of the
most famous images of the Great Depression.

CHAPTER THREE

The Great Depression

*When I was working with people who were
strangers to me, being disabled gave me an
immense advantage. People are kinder to you.
It puts you on a different level than if you go
into a situation whole and secure.*
—Dorothea Lange

Dorothea Lange and her family were living in San Francisco on October 24, 1929, when the fast pace of the Roaring Twenties came to a stop. The overheated stock market crashed. Stock holdings that had been valued at thousands of dollars one day were worthless the next. Once-wealthy investors, bankers, and business owners saw their fortunes disappear within days.

By the early 1930s, several million people were unemployed. Factories closed. Banks failed, leaving depositors with nothing. Masses of unemployed men wandered the nation's roads and railroads, hoping to find enough pickup work to exchange for a meal. The American people had never lived in such fear and doubt. Earlier, they had come to believe, as President Hoover had said, that the nation had conquered poverty forever. Instead, the economic depression deepened, gripping the country and most of the industrialized world with frightening suddenness. Throughout history, hard work and thrift had been the keys to security, if not always wealth. But now, people found their lives changed by economic forces they could neither control nor understand.

The Great Depression, as this period of economic struggle became known, affected Lange and Dixon, as well as their friends and the people who paid for her photo portraits and his paintings. While the couple never went hungry, they had a hard time making ends meet.

This fear and insecurity affected the couple's relationship. In addition, Dixon's health was declining. His heavy smoking had led to emphysema (a serious lung disease), so that even the slightest exertion left him out of breath and panting. He and Lange quarreled more often and even tried living apart. Sometimes the boys were with them; other times they were at boarding school or living with friends. Nothing seemed to help, and the couple drifted farther apart.

For a time, Lange kept her studio fairly busy with clients who wanted portraits and still had plenty of money. However, she found herself increasingly troubled by the street scenes unfolding outside her studio. Unemployed men of all ages wandered the streets, many of their faces expressing fear, despair, or anger.

One day, without quite knowing why, she grabbed her camera and headed to Market Street, where she knew that a woman called the "White Angel" operated a soup kitchen—a place where people could get a free meal of stew, bread, and a mug of coffee. She didn't know how the men would react to her and her camera, so she took her brother, Martin, with her for protection. But, lost in their own thoughts, the men paid little attention to the woman photographer.

White Angel Bread Line

When the Great Depression began, there were no government programs to help people who had no work and no money, even if they were ill or disabled. The only help available came from a few city programs and private or religious charities. These sources were soon overwhelmed by the need, and money became increasingly scarce. The men Lange saw at the soup kitchen seemed to be facing lives with no future prospects. The despair was etched in deep lines in their faces.

Using a 3- by 4-inch (7.6- by 10-centimeter) Graflex camera, Lange took twelve pictures that day, three of them at the White Angel's soup kitchen. One of these showed a man with his elbow on a rail, a battered tin bowl, a crumpled hat, and his down-turned mouth telling a story without words. She called the picture "White Angel Bread Line."

Lange had no way of knowing then that this first photograph from her first day of working in the streets would become one of the most famous pictures of the Depression. She was focusing more and more on documentary photography—pictures designed to convey a message. As photography writer George P. Elliott has stated, "This image ["White Angel Bread Line"] does not derive its power from formal elegance so much as from its being inextricably entangled with the comment it is mak-

"San Francisco Social Security Office." Dorothea Lange, 1937

At the Social Security Office in San Francisco, men lined up for the first unemployment checks issued by the state. They received from $6 to $15 per week for up to sixteen weeks.

ing. It is art for life's sake." With this and her other Depression photographs, Lange was beginning to put a human face on the suffering of the Depression.

Lange did not know what to do with her new photographs, other than to put them on her studio wall. Her portrait patrons were troubled by the pictures and turned away. But a group of San Francisco Bay Area photographers, who had just started a

"Man Sleeping in Parking Lot." Dorothea Lange, c. 1934

There seems to be no comfort or softness for this homeless man. Lange called this photo "Man Sleeping in Parking Lot."

photography gallery in Oakland, recognized that her photographs made an unusually powerful statement. Lange was not interested in joining the group, but she was pleased that they wanted to display the pictures. Those first prints gave her a new kind of fame.

A New Deal

In 1933, as Lange continued to prowl the streets of San Francisco, the nation began a dramatic new approach to solving the problems of the Great Depression when Franklin Delano Roosevelt took office as president of the United States. He followed Herbert Hoover, who had insisted that the Depression would end without government interference. By contrast, Roosevelt promised a "New Deal for all Americans." During his first months in office—a period known as the Hundred Days—the new president proposed a radical program of action. He believed that the government should try to help the millions of Americans who were trapped in unemployment and poverty. There also were programs to aid business and banks. The day after Roosevelt took office, he closed every bank in the country; bank examiners were to reopen each bank when they decided it was strong enough.

A willing Congress quickly passed all of Roosevelt's proposals. The programs of the Hundred Days provided relief from some of the hunger, unemployment, and fear. Thousands of men and women found temporary work on projects funded by the government. Over a period of ten years, for example, more than 2 million young men went to work for the Civilian Conservation Corps (CCC). They worked in parks and forests, while living in army-style camps. They built picnic areas and campgrounds, fought fires, and planted trees. Part of their monthly pay was sent home or placed in bank accounts.

Programs like the CCC provided help, hope, and confidence. All the ambitious New Deal experiments, however, could not cure the underlying economic and social problems that had plunged the nation into the Great Depression. Roosevelt tried new ideas throughout the 1930s, but only the approach of World War II (1939–1945) and the resulting demand for a massive military buildup would return America to full employment.

A Great Team

In 1934, Paul Schuster Taylor, an economist at the University of California at Berkeley, saw Lange's photos at the photographers' gallery in Oakland. Taylor had just begun a series of studies of migratory workers for a new state agency called the State

Roosevelt drew huge crowds when he ran for the presidency.

Emergency Relief Administration (SERA). SERA officials wanted Taylor to report on the problems faced by the thousands of farmworkers, including families, pouring into California.

Taylor wanted to convince the officials of the need for vigorous action. He knew his reports would have to be very persuasive, since few outsiders had any idea of the suffering in the labor camps or how the people were being exploited by the farm man-

ROOSEVELT AND POLIO

Lange observed Franklin Delano Roosevelt's election victory and his presidency with special interest because he, too, was a victim of polio. In 1921, when Roosevelt was in his late thirties and in the midst of his political career, he was stricken by the disease, which left him with both legs completely paralyzed.

That seemed to mark the end of Roosevelt's political career. But the support and energy of his wife, Eleanor, plus his own remarkable determination, enabled him to return to politics. He never regained the use of his legs, but by building up his upper body, he gained enough strength to stand with the help of heavy steel braces.

The fact that Roosevelt did not let his severe disability destroy his career must have been heartening to Lange. Many people felt that his suffering made him compassionate toward their own hardships. From Lange's own experience, she wrote, "When I was working with people who were strangers to me, being disabled gave me an immense advantage. People are kinder to you. It puts you on a different level than if you go into a situation whole and secure."

This 1930 photo is one of the few that shows President Roosevelt's heavy leg braces.

agers. He also was aware that photographs would make his argument far more convincing.

Taylor asked Lange to work with him. They would tour the state's rural areas, preparing the reports together, making heavy use of her photos. Lange agreed. She was now a documentary photographer, being paid for her work. In fact, however, she was

THE BEGINNINGS OF DOCUMENTARY PHOTOGRAPHY

The aim of documentary photography is to present facts as vividly as possible, often with a purpose: to arouse fear, sympathy, or anger in order to spur people or the government to take action.

Documentary photography came into being as soon as photography was invented. The American Civil War (1861–1865), only a few years after photography emerged, inspired a number of photographers to document the conflict—to make an accurate and vivid record of events. For example, Mathew Brady, a well-known portrait photographer, formed a team of about twenty camera reporters to roam the battlefields.

These early photojournalists labored under severe handicaps. Each picture began with a square glass plate that had to be coated with an emulsion and then inserted into a big, box-like camera. After exposure, the glass negative had to be developed right away, so every photographer traveled with a horse-drawn darkroom or a tent. Another problem was that it took about twenty minutes to make an exposure. Any movement created a blur on the photograph. This meant that no action pictures were possible. With a few blurred exceptions, all Civil War photos were taken just before or after the fighting took place.

Cameras were improving in the late nineteenth and early twentieth centuries, but there still were severe limitations for the documentary photographer. In the 1880s, for example, Jacob Riis, a police photographer, wanted to show the filthy, unhealthy conditions in New York City's slums. His book, *How the Other Half Lives* (1890), containing pictures and text, was a powerful indictment of slumlords and corrupt officials. However, the impact was somewhat limited because new techniques of copying photographs in books had not yet been perfected. The result was that, in Riis's book, the pictures were not as clear and powerful as the original photographs.

Despite these early difficulties, Riis is regarded as one of the great pioneers of documentary photography. He was one of the first to show the power of photography as a weapon for social change.

In 1890 Jacob Riis published one of the first books of documentary photography, which exposed the poverty and living conditions of New York City.

hired to work as a "typist," because state officials could not understand why Taylor could possibly need a photographer for reports on farm labor.

Taylor's and Lange's travels through California, and the reports they prepared, turned out to be a remarkable learning experience—for Lange, for state and federal government officials, and for everyone who encountered their first published work. Every day, from dawn to dusk, often skipping meals, the two toured labor camps that the growers had constructed. While Taylor interviewed workers, Lange was busy with her camera. Soon, she was helping with the interviews and the written reports, too.

Lange had to overcome her own shyness in order to walk into a camp and start taking pictures. She approached people slowly, sometimes talking to them about herself. She never intruded on their privacy, and, at the first hint that someone did not want to be photographed, she quietly backed off.

The influence of Lange's documentary photographs would soon reach much farther than she had imagined. She was about to become one of the most famous photographers of the Great Depression.

Lange caught the irony of two migrant workers
who could not possibly "relax" by riding the train.

Opposite: Lange's photos of migrant families captured
the expressions of people who had reached rock bottom.

Lange captured this Missouri farmer and his wife, who stare into the distance, dazed by the enormity of facing their new life as migrant workers.

CHAPTER FOUR

Photographer of the People

I had to get my camera to register the things about those people that were more important than how poor they were—their pride, their strength, their spirit.
—Dorothea Lange

In 1934 and 1935, Dorothea Lange's fame spread, beginning with the reports she and Taylor put together about conditions in California's rural areas. Everywhere they went they saw lives ruined by the Great Depression. Entire families were destitute. They lived in makeshift shelters, their clothes slowly turning to rags. Children went to bed hungry, and some starved. Medical help was rarely available.

One of the great revelations of their first trip was learning about the Dust Bowl in the Great Plains states and the terrible impact it had on farms and farm families there. Lange found these "Okies" harder to photograph than the unemployed of San Francisco. "Their roots were all torn out," she recalled. "The only background they had was a background of utter poverty. It's very hard to photograph a proud man against a background like that, because it doesn't show what he's proud about." She then revealed her most important goal in documenting the impact of the Depression: "I had to get my camera to register the things about those people that were more important than how poor they were—their pride, their strength, their spirit."

After she returned home from that trip, Lange and Dixon made one last attempt to patch up their marriage. She was now forty, and he was sixty-two; they had been married for fifteen years. They rented a new apartment in San Francisco and brought the two boys home. Nothing seemed to help, however.

In addition, as Lange continued to work and travel with Paul Taylor, the two realized that they were in love. She immediately told Dixon, and they agreed to a divorce. Taylor also ended an unhappy marriage.

Dorothea Lange and Paul Taylor were married in December 1935. For the next thirty years—until Dorothea's death in 1965—the couple lived happy, productive lives together.

Photographer—Field Investigator

In the meantime, the Taylor-Lange partnership had had remarkable success. Their report on conditions in California labor camps was sent to Washington, D.C. In large

THE DUST BOWL

During the boom days on the Great Plains in the early 1900s, farmers planted wheat and corn wherever they could. They cut down trees and tore up lawns to plant more. There was nothing left to hold the soil in place when a series of droughts hit the region in the early 1930s. The soil turned to dust, and the wind blew it in huge "dust storms" that swept across the continent, finally dropping tons of what had been fertile topsoil into the Atlantic Ocean.

By 1934, much of the Great Plains had become a wasteland, referred to as the Dust Bowl. Thousands of people who could no longer make a living on the land piled their belongings in—and on top of—beat-up old cars and trucks. Most headed west for California, where farming was a year-round activity. The first few hundred families found work as migrant pickers or planters.

Soon, however, there were far more migrants than jobs, and many wandered the roads aimlessly. State officials, and most people, had little idea of what was going on and had not even heard of the Dust Bowl. Lange wrote about her first encounter with these newcomers when she watched a family in a crowded car at a gasoline station:

They looked very woebegone to me. They were American whites. I looked at the license plate on the car and it was Oklahoma. I got out and asked which way they were going, were they looking for work? And they said, "We've been blown out." I questioned what they meant, and they told me about the dust storm. They were the first arrivals that I saw. . . . All of that day, driving for the next three or four hundred miles, I saw these people.

Lange and Taylor were stunned by their first
encounters with refugees from the Dust Bowl.

part because of this report, a new federal agency, the Federal Emergency Relief Administration, provided money to build two camps for migrant workers in northern California. While there was some opposition from growers and from state and local officials, the two camps represented an important beginning. They offered the workers a chance to manage their own living places. The camps also were the first housing projects ever financed by the federal government.

In August 1935, Lange began a new job. Another economist, Roy Stryker, was working in the newly formed Resettlement Administration (RA) in Washington, D.C.; he had the rather vague title Chief of the Historical Division. The RA had been created to find ways of combating rural poverty. Stryker hired Lange to be part of

Few Americans knew of the devastation caused by the
Dust Bowl until photographs like this were published.

"Huge dark dust clouds swarm over houses in rural Colorado." Dorothea Lange, 1935

what was probably the greatest team of photographers ever assembled. Their work would inform the public about the government's relief and rebuilding programs.

Lange's job title was Photographer—Field Investigator, with a salary of $2,300 a year. Taylor becaome a regional labor adviser for the RA, working out of the same office as Lange. In 1937, the RA was renamed the Farm Security Administration (FSA). Lange continued to be based in California, the only person on Stryker's team who did not work in Washington, D.C.

Americans in the twenty-first century can easily recognize that Dorothea Lange's photographs are excellent, but it is more difficult to understand how special her work appeared to people during the Depression. From 1935 to 1939, Lange worked with Stryker's unit along with his other photographers, exploring the rural areas of California as well as states of the Southwest. Her images were used in newspapers throughout the country and in magazines and journals, as well as in the reports produced by Stryker's office.

From the beginning, Lange's pictures stood out as exceptional. One of the earliest reviews of her work, by Willard Van Dyke, appeared in fall 1934. Here is part of his review:

> Dorothea Lange has turned to the people of the American Scene with the intention of making an adequate photographic record of them. These people are in the midst of great changes—contemporary problems are reflected in their faces, a tremendous drama is unfolding before them, and Dorothea Lange is photographing it through them. . . .
>
> In an old Ford she drives to a place most likely to yield subjects consistent with her general sympathies. Unlike the newspaper reporter, she has no news or editorial policies to direct her movements; it is only her deeply personal sympathies for the unfortunates, the downtrodden, the misfits among her contemporaries that provide the impetus for her expedition. She may park her car at the waterfront during a strike, perhaps at a meeting of unemployed, by sleepers in the city square, at transient shelters—breadlines, parades, or demonstrations. Here she waits with her camera open and unconcealed, her mind ready.

A few months later, the great nature photographer Ansel Adams saw a display of her photos. He also was amazed:

From the beginning, Lange and Taylor made an outstanding team. His writing complemented her photographs.

On the Texas plains, Taylor photographed Lange using her Graflex from her favorite picture-taking spot.

Lange let people's faces tell the story of their hardships.

She is an extraordinary phenomenon in photography. She is both a humanitarian and an artist. Her pictures of people show an uncanny perception, which is transmitted with immense impact on the spectator. To my mind, she presents the almost perfect balance between artist and human being. . . . Her pictures are both records of actuality and exquisitely sensitive emotional documents. Her pictures tell you of many things; they tell you these things with conviction, directness, completeness. There is never propaganda. . . . If any documents of this turbulent age are justified to endure, the photographs of Dorothea Lange shall most certainly.

Stryker too found Lange's work different and special in a way that was new to him. Compared to the photos taken by the rest of his outstanding staff, Stryker felt that Lange's photos "had the most sensitivity and the most rapport with people."

Several years later, in 1941, photographer and filmmaker Pare Lorentz wrote:

[She] was a little, soft-voiced, bright-eyed woman with a weather-beaten face . . . beret cocked over one ear . . . stalking the back roads of the country photographing the poor. . . . She has selected them with an unerring eye. You do not find in her portrait gallery the bindle stiffs [hoboes], the drifters, the tramps, the unfortunate, aimless dregs of the country. Her people stand straight and look you in the eye. They have the simple dignity of people who have leaned against the wind, and worked in the sun and owned their land.

Lorentz's description echoes Lange's desire to photograph people's "pride, their strength, their spirit." Stryker too sought that same positive spirit in all FSA work. "When anyone said that the FSA photographs were all depressing," Stryker recalled, "I say look again. You see the set of that chin. You see the way that mother stands. You

"Migratory woman, Greek, living in a cotton camp near Exeter, California." Dorothea Lange, 1937

Lange's photos also showed people's strength and determination.

see the straight line of that man's shoulders. You see something in those faces that transcends misery."

Lange took her single most famous photograph in 1936. Returning home from field work on a rainy March day, she saw a handwritten sign saying simply, "Pea-Pickers Camp." She kept on driving but couldn't get the sign out of her mind. "Having convinced myself that I could continue on," she recalled, "I did the opposite. Almost without realizing what I was doing, I made a U-turn on the empty highway. . . . I was following instinct, not reason; I drove into that wet and soggy camp and parked my car like a homing pigeon."

She slowly approached a woman and her children, talking softly as she advanced. She took five exposures, each a little closer to the family's lean-to. Lange learned that they had been living on vegetables that froze in the fields and birds the children managed to kill by throwing rocks. "She had just sold the tires from her car to buy food. . . . She seemed to know that my pictures might help her and so she helped me."

And they did help. Lange gave the photographs and her report to a San Francisco newspaper, urging fast action. News wire services picked them up and spread the story nationwide. Federal officials responded by sending an emergency shipment of food to the stricken region.

The final exposure of the thirty-two-year-old "Migrant Mother" soon took on a life of its own. It was reproduced countless times and is generally considered one of the nation's greatest photographs. "I don't understand it," Lange said. "I don't know why. It seems to me that I see things as good as that all the time."

During her years with the FSA, Lange and Taylor settled into family life in Berkeley, across the bay from San Francisco. They rented a large, airy house in the hills above the university. They now had five children: Lange's two boys, Daniel, who was ten, and John, seven; and Taylor's three—two girls, ages thirteen and six, and a son who was ten.

Combining family life and career was now even more complicated and stressful than it had been with Dixon. As she had done in the past, Lange frequently sent the children to stay with friends. On weekends, she usually brought all five children home.

Lange was now so determined to pursue her career that she became increasingly difficult to live with. The children found her humorless and demanding most of the time. Behind her back they called her "Dictator Dot."

Paul Taylor understood that his wife was actually a kind and caring person. He knew that much of her antagonistic behavior was the result of the enormous stress she lived with. His understanding made him forgiving toward her, and he tried to help the children accept her behavior as well.

The strains in Lange's life were incredible. When she was on the road, with Taylor or alone, she often worked fifteen hours a day, before collapsing in an auto camp (an early form of motel) and having a makeshift meal. Back home, she labored in her darkroom from early morning until ten or eleven at night. The long-term stress began to show with sharp stomach pains—the beginning of gastrointestinal troubles that steadily worsened every year, eventually turning into the cancer that would claim her life.

THE FSA PHOTOGRAPHERS

Roy Stryker's FSA group included some of the country's most famous photographers. They were all young, with Dorothea Lange the oldest, at forty. Other outstanding talents included Ben Shahn, who was well-known for his painting and murals; Walker Evans, a brilliant photographer, who took a leave in 1936 to work with James Agee to produce the book *Let Us Now Praise Famous Men* describing the living and working conditions of Alabama sharecroppers; and Arthur Rothstein, fresh out of college, who took very dramatic and powerful photographs of rural conditions, especially in the Dust Bowl.

The combined talents of these people, plus a handful of others who worked for Stryker, produced a remarkable record of the impact of the Great Depression on rural and small-town America. The photographs were offered free to newspapers, magazines, and book authors. Some books were composed of FSA photographs and text, such as Archibald MacLeish's *Land of the Free* (1938) and Sherwood Anderson's *Home Town* (1941). Two of the greatest FSA narrative books were the Evans and Agee collection and one by Lange and her husband, Paul Taylor, *An American Exodus* (1939). When the FSA was disbanded in 1942, Stryker turned over to the Library of Congress about 70,000 prints and 170,000 negatives.

One reason for the great success of the FSA work was the importance of documentary photography in the 1930s. There was no television then and, except for brief movie newsreels, people had no visual images of what was happening during these years of economic upheaval and change.

In a way, however, the FSA photographs do not give an accurate picture of Depression America. They do show the suffering and economic upheaval. But conditions in the 1930s also produced anger and despair. These emotions do not emerge from the photographs. Instead, most of the images show us the strength, courage, and determination of the American people.

"Migrant agricultural worker's family." Dorothea Lange, 1936

To take her "Migrant Mother" photograph, Lange began with this long-range shot, hoping to gain the woman's confidence.

Another source of strain was Lange's stormy relationship with Stryker. He recognized that she was the most skilled of the FSA photographers, but he also found her to be stubborn and troublesome. It was hard enough to communicate across the continent; they had to rely on mail because the telephone was too expensive. Lange was constantly asking for money—money to pay for darkroom supplies or film or a small salary for an assistant. Stryker did his best, but he became increasingly frustrated with his star photographer.

Despite Lange's difficulties, she retained her enthusiasm for her work. From fall to spring, while Taylor was teaching at the University of California at Berkeley, she traveled up and down the farm areas of California. She hired Ron Partridge, the son of

Opposite: "Migrant Mother"—one of several shots Lange took.

close friends, as her assistant, and paid him a dollar a day out of her meager expense allowance of $4 a day.

During the summers of 1937, 1938, and 1939, Lange and Taylor toured the South for the FSA. They drove thousands of miles, sometimes through droughts or floods, documenting the life of tenant farmers and of the shrinking numbers who still owned their own farms.

In the West, she had observed thousands of migrants searching for seasonal farm work. In the South, most people stayed where they were. The old plantation system had collapsed in the decades following the American Civil War. Freed slaves, as well as white farm owners who could no longer sell enough cotton, became sharecroppers or tenant farmers. They worked for the plantation owners in exchange for a share of their crop. Often, when the accounts were settled, the tenants and sharecroppers found they did not even break even and had to borrow from the owner to get by until the next harvest. In addition, while the Great Plains had been devastated by the droughts that created Dust Bowl conditions, the Southeast had been stricken by three years of heavy rains and floods.

As in the West, Lange's photographs and Taylor's writing provided dramatic accounts that persuaded large segments of the public, as well as government officials, of the need for relief. By the late 1930s, other photographers and writers also were documenting Depression conditions. They were joined by a variety of scholars, including historians, economists, and anthropologists, who were trying to understand what had happened to the American Dream and what could be done to restore it.

In spring 1939, the publication of John Steinbeck's novel *The Grapes of Wrath* shocked the nation. The dramatic account of Tom Joad and his family brought home the suffering of the Great Depression in a personal way that not even the best photographs could achieve. The creation of the movie version, which was begun two months later, added the power of film.

An American Exodus

As others had done, Lange and Taylor had been assembling material for a book of their own, which would combine his writing and her photographs. After months of disappointment in mid-1939, they finally received a book contract, only to have publication threatened by two catastrophic events, one global, one personal.

First, on September 1, 1939, German dictator Adolph Hitler launched an invasion of Poland, plunging Europe and then the world into World War II. Although the United States did not enter the conflict until December 1941, the nation began a

"Ex-slave with a long memory." Dorothea Lange, 1938

Lange's photographs of tenant farmers in the South included this picture of a woman who had been born a slave.

massive military buildup. Factories and shipyards started hiring workers. Within months, full employment returned, the economy was humming, and the Great Depression was becoming a painful memory. For Lange and Taylor, the question was: In these changed circumstances, would the public still be interested in a book about the impact of the Depression on rural America?

The second catastrophe, this time personal, was a letter from Stryker, informing

DOROTHEA LANGE AND JOHN STEINBECK

Many people have wondered about the possible influence of Dorothea Lange's photographs on John Steinbeck's outstanding novel *The Grapes of Wrath* and the film based on this novel. The two did not meet until after publication of the book. Nevertheless, there is good evidence of a connection.

First, in 1937, a nonprofit organization had received permission to publish a pamphlet containing several of Lange's photos along with articles that Steinbeck had written for a San Francisco newspaper. The pamphlet was distributed widely and reprinted four times.

Second, many people have noticed striking similarities between some of Lange's photos of individuals and Steinbeck's description of certain characters. Writer D.G. Kehl carefully analyzed several photos and showed how closely they resembled Steinbeck's detailed personality studies. In addition, when shooting of the film began, director John Ford used Lange's photos for background.

Writer Pare Lorentz gave credit to both Lange and Steinbeck for the displaced farm families gaining better conditions: "Lange, with her still pictures that have been reproduced in thousands of newspapers, and in magazines and Sunday supplements, and Steinbeck, with two novels, a play, and a motion picture, have done more for these tragic nomads than all the politicians in the country."

John Steinbeck

Lange that her position would be terminated as of January 1, 1940. She had campaigned vigorously for her position almost from the start, even offering to work without a salary. Lange was fond of the FSA and admired Stryker, in addition to loving her work. She was devastated by the loss of the job.

Considering the fact that Lange was widely regarded as the outstanding photographer of the Depression, it was hard for people—Lange included—to understand why he had chosen to drop her from his staff. Stryker argued that he did it because of his constantly shrinking budget and the expense of working with her across the continent. None of his reasons seemed adequate. Many observers concluded that Stryker simply found Lange too difficult to deal with.

In spite of these problems, the Lange-Taylor book, *An American Exodus*, was published on schedule in January 1940. Somewhat surprisingly, Stryker worked hard to promote the book, sending copies to influential government officials, including First Lady Eleanor Roosevelt, and paying for advertising. The work was well received by the critics. Here are a few examples:

The Nation: "Both the text and the photographs are excellent; together they provide a vivid story . . . of the nature and extent of the disaster."

The New Republic: "*An American Exodus* could scarcely have been improved upon. . . . The photographs of Dorothea Lange are beyond praise; indeed they are so good that the text is really not essential."

Time: "Some of the photographs are exceedingly good; some are merely 'magnificent'."

Although the reviews were impressive and must have pleased Lange and Taylor, the book never sold well. As they had feared, people no longer wanted to think about the Dust Bowl or the Great Depression.

Throughout 1940, Lange did some freelance work for another Department of Agriculture agency. She now had time to focus on her home life, including a spacious Berkeley house she and Taylor had purchased. This was to be her home for the remaining twenty-five years of her life. Descriptions of the new home by friends reveal a more mellow side to Lange. She had an interior decorator's skill and frequently rearranged the décor. She loved to cook and entertained often. Her relationship with the five children seemed to be better, too, and she taught some of them how to cook.

She also had time to pursue a new dream: Lange applied for a Guggenheim Fellowship that would provide the money and time to develop a more scholarly approach to her photography. She submitted her application in October 1940. The following spring, she learned that she had been awarded the prestigious fellowship.

The Japanese attack on Pearl Harbor shocked
Americans. The demand for isolation from the
world was replaced by an eagerness to strike back.

CHAPTER FIVE

The Troubled War Years— and After

[Dorothea Lange] functioned in effect as our national eye of conscience in the internment camps. Her constant concerns—[including] the survival of human dignity under impossible conditions . . . were perfectly suited to the subject.
—*A.D. Coleman*

Throughout the 1930s, the American people and Congress steadfastly refused to become involved in events beyond U.S. borders. Even in 1940, when Hitler's powerful military swept through much of Europe, and Japan was conquering an empire in Asia and the Pacific islands, the demand for isolation remained strong.

On December 7, 1941, the Japanese attacked the U.S. naval base at Pearl Harbor in the Hawaiian Islands. The surprise attack, which killed more than 2,000 Americans and destroyed most of the U.S. military's Pacific fleet, changed everything. Overnight, the American people were united and determined to fight back against both Japan and the Germany-Italy alliance.

While the nation rushed to mobilize for war in 1942, the Japanese continued to advance, invading the American territory of the Philippines and easily capturing U.S. islands in the Pacific. In Europe, the Germans and Italians seemed poised to invade England.

In the early weeks of 1942, a combination of anger and fear swept the American West Coast. Rumors that Japanese aircraft had been spotted over San Francisco convinced many that the Japanese were about to invade California. There were more than 100,000 people of Japanese descent living in the state, and the fear grew that they would aid an invading force. As the fear intensified, there were increasing demands that everyone of Japanese descent be rounded up and placed in detention

Tom Clark, future Supreme Court justice, said the internment of Japanese Americans was "all the result of racism and wartime hysteria."

centers. Many agreed with a San Francisco newspaper columnist who wrote, "Herd 'em up, pack 'em off. Let 'em be pinched, hurt and hungry." Congressman John Rankin of Mississippi was even more outspoken: "I'm for catching every Japanese in America, Alaska, and Hawaii now and putting them in concentration camps. . . . Damn them! Let's get rid of them."

On February 19, 1942, President Franklin Delano Roosevelt gave in to the urging of his advisors and issued Executive Order 9066. It required the U.S. Army to move all people of Japanese descent to temporary centers until camps could be built for them far inland, away from the coast and from urban or industrial centers.

While many Americans paid little attention to the order, and many more approved of it, others were stunned by the heavy-handed disregard of people's constitutional rights. Lange and Taylor were both outraged. They argued that the United States was also at war with Germany and Italy, but nothing was being done to Americans of German or Italian descent.

Lange faced a conflict when a new civilian agency—the War Relocation Authority (WRA)—was set up to operate the camps, and she was asked to document the agency's work. At first, she felt she was violating her beliefs, but Paul persuaded her that it would be good to make an accurate record of events.

"Japanese Americans assemble at the Van Ness Avenue control station for evacuation." Dorothea Lange, 1942

As she traveled with the bewildered evacuees, Lange observed that the camps "are what happens to us if we lose our heads."

Lange had won her Guggenheim fellowship the year before and had started her research. But she had to stop abruptly when her brother, Martin, was arrested for a scheme to defraud the state of California. The episode was so painful for Lange that she couldn't bring herself to explain to the Guggenheim people why she was putting her work on hold. After Martin was convicted and given a short prison sentence, she started again on her cherished Guggenheim work early in 1942. A month later, the WRA assignment again forced her to suspend the fellowship work.

"Turlock, California. These young evacuees of Japanese ancestry are awaiting their turn for baggage." Dorothea Lange, 1942

According to critic A.D. Coleman, one of Lange's unique skills was photographing "the helpless innocence of children."

Lange made three visits to the relocation camp at Manzanar in California's Owens Valley.

To the Camps

The Japanese were ordered to report to relocation centers for the duration of the war. Of the 110,000 people involved, two-thirds were Nisei—children born in the United States, which made them American citizens. The rest were Isei—immigrants who had been born in Japan and were not citizens.

The people of Japanese descent had been model residents and citizens since they began arriving in the mid-1800s. In spite of often violent discrimination against them, they had built remarkably successful farms, businesses, and shops.

Suddenly, they were regarded as the enemy and forced to leave for what were essentially prison camps. These camps were located in remote areas, from the Rocky Mountains and the California desert to the swamps of Arkansas. "We had only 48 hours to get out of our homes," one Nisei recalled. "They came in truckloads to buy our things. We had to get rid of our furniture and appliances for whatever the people would pay. They took terrible advantage of us."

Lange began photographing the hapless people as they boarded buses and trains for relocation. From April to July, she traveled with them. The internment camps were surrounded by barbed wire with guard towers at the corners.

Most people remained in the overcrowded camps for more than three years. Some camps held 10,000 people in more than 450 tar-paper-covered barracks, with community toilets and showers and a large mess hall. Some camp residents had to cope with summer heat of 120 degrees Fahrenheit (49 degrees Celsius), while others faced winter cold of minus 30 degrees F (–34 degrees C).

Lange found that the detainees accepted her as a friendly presence. The U.S. Army was a different story. Wherever she went, an army officer followed her. She was often accused of spying for anti-army groups, and dozens of her photographs and negatives were confiscated.

The Japanese Americans organized camp life with great efficiency. Children attended classes and a variety of activities. Adults managed the camp, arranged social events, and developed projects to aid the war effort. At some camps, they planted trees, and, in every camp, they grew fruits and vegetables. At a Wyoming camp, they used irrigation to reclaim 2,700 acres of desert. More than 1,000 young men volunteered for military service, while their parents remained in the camps. The Nisei 442nd Regimental Combat Team, fighting in Italy, suffered more casualties and won more medals than any other army combat brigade in history.

While working on the WRA assignment, Lange experienced more of the sharp stomach pains that had troubled her before. On some days, the pain was so severe that she could not work. Doctors were unsure of the cause, so after a day or two of rest, she went back to work.

The best opportunity to assess her internment photos came thirty years later, in 1972, when some of them were shown in an exhibit organized by her former assistant, Richard Conrat, and his wife, Maisie. The traveling exhibit contained sixty-three images, dominated by twenty-seven of Lange's photographs. The exhibit was then put in book form by the Conrats, with the title *Executive Order 9066: The Internment of 110,000 Japanese Americans*. Reviews were enthusiastic. As critic A.D. Coleman wrote:

> She was precisely the right photographer for the job. . . . She functioned in effect as our national eye of conscience in the internment camps. Her con-

Paul Taylor said that the photographs by Lange and her colleagues could "remind people that the evacuees were not convicted, were not found guilty of anything, that they were entitled to every consideration under the American principle of fair play."

stant concerns—[including] the survival of human dignity under impossible conditions . . . were perfectly suited to the subject. . . . [Some of] her most poignant and angry images were made for the WRA.

In the words of Hilton Kramer, art critic for *The New York Times*:

[The exhibit was] harrowing in its vivid glimpses of Americans suddenly made refugees and prisoners in their own country. It . . . reminds one of how

The Troubled War Years—and After   **65**

FREEDOM . . . AND APOLOGIES

In 1944, the Supreme Court upheld the policy of Japanese American internment in the case of *Korematsu v. United States*. Justice Frank Murphy dissented. The exclusion order, he said, "toppled into the ugly abyss of racism."

Nearly forty years later, in 1983, U.S. District Judge Marilyn Hall Patel ruled that the evacuation had been "based upon unsubstantiated facts [and] distortions." She warned that the government must "protect all citizens from the . . . prejudices so easily stirred up" by war. In the same year, a congressional committee studied the internment and concluded that a "grave injustice" had been done to Japanese Americans because of "race prejudice, war hysteria, and a failure of political leadership."

In 1988, Congress voted to issue a formal apology to Japanese Americans and granted a payment of $20,000 to each of the estimated 60,000 survivors.

"Children of the Weill public school, from the so-called international settlement, shown in a flag pledge ceremony." Dorothea Lange, 1942

"Everything they could possibly do for themselves, they did," Lange noted, including teaching the children to be good citizens.

"Women line up for paychecks–Richmond Shipyards." Dorothea Lange, c. 1943

Workers at the massive Richmond, California, shipyards found that racial segregation had ended during the war.

powerful the photographic medium has been in recording the political horrors of the modern age. . . . Miss Lange's work dominated the exhibition. Her pictures of the Japanese internment are, in a sense, a further extension of her work in the thirties. . . . She and her colleagues have left us a moving and permanent record of a human and political catastrophe—something that no other medium could have done in quite this way, with quite this effect.

To the Shipyards

After her work on the internment, Lange began a series of photographic studies of ethnic minorities in the San Francisco Bay area for the Office of War Information (OWI). In this project, too, the U.S. Army monitored her closely. When she photographed Italian American families in San Francisco, for example, her pictures were scrutinized for anything—such as the topography of the city—that might be useful to the enemy.

In 1943, Lange worked with the famous photographer, Ansel Adams, on an assignment for *Fortune* magazine, photographing life in the shipyards at Richmond, not far from Berkeley. During the war, Richmond became one of many wartime boomtowns. Many of the migrant workers found high-paying jobs in the shipyards, where new ships were being constructed with record speed. Men and women from all parts of the country found work in Richmond and at the aircraft plants in southern California.

Thousands of African Americans joined this westward movement. They discovered that the necessities of war created a suspension of racial discrimination. For the duration of the war, they were able to work alongside whites and even live in the same apartment buildings, which was unusual at that time.

By late 1943, the shipyards at Richmond were the largest in the world. A town of a few thousand had to find living space for more than 200,000 new workers. The government built 25,000 new housing units, but it was not enough. Lange found families living in tents and garages, in addition to overcrowded apartments and rooming houses. The shipyards operated twenty-four hours a day, the men and women working in three eight-hour shifts. The workers put up with the overcrowding, the high price of housing, and the constant breakdown of services, such as sewers and garbage removal. These hardships were nothing compared to the Depression years, and most had never dreamed of making so much money.

Dorothea Lange and Ansel Adams were photography's odd couple. They arrived in his station wagon. Adams, with his bushy beard and ten-gallon hat, set up big tripod cameras, lights, and a platform to photograph from. He took photographs of the overall scene, although he was constantly surrounded by curious workers. Lange, meantime, melted into the crowds, her small camera hardly noticed.

Late in the war, as Lange was finishing her work for OWI, her health grew steadily worse, but she remained determined to document the tremendous social and economic changes taking place. "You can't deny what you must do," she said, "no matter what it costs."

Failing Health—and More Work

In April 1945, Lange was asked to photograph the San Francisco conference that launched the United Nations. Against the advice of her doctors, she took the assignment. Government restrictions hampered her again, however; she could see the delegates only from a great distance, making her kind of photography impossible. Frustrated, she went out into the streets, and settled for photographing the delegates wherever she found them.

In August 1945, the month the war ended, Lange's pains became so severe that she

On her travels with Taylor, Lange continued to capture the humanity of individuals, such as this young man in front of the Taj Mahal in India, just as she had done during the Great Depression.

needed morphine for some relief. She was operated on for gallbladder disease, but that was not the cause of the pain, and it only made things worse. A month later, she began bleeding internally and was rushed back to the hospital. Her family and friends thought this was the end. "It was a terrible time," her husband Paul Taylor said. "We thought we had lost her."

For the next few months, Lange was in and out of the hospital, and throughout 1946, she spent nearly all her time at home. She read and did a little gardening and sewing, but she was not able to work. She wrote to her Guggenheim contact early in 1947, saying she hoped to resume work soon. Five years later, she tried again. But her continuing poor health prevented her from ever finishing the fellowship she had begun with such high hopes in 1941.

Health problems continued to plague Lange. She was operated on for bleeding ulcers in 1946, and, while this provided some relief from the stomach pain and nau-

EDWARD STEICHEN AND THE FAMILY OF MAN

Edward Steichen was one of the great photographers of the twentieth century. His early photographs helped to establish the medium as an art form. In the 1920s and 1930s, his portraits of personalities, such as Greta Garbo and Charlie Chaplin, added to his fame. During World War II, he supervised all naval combat photography and produced a film, *The Fighting Lady* (1944).

In 1947, Steichen became director of photography for the Museum of Modern Art. A great admirer of Dorothea Lange, he developed two famous exhibitions that included her pictures. For a show about the Great Depression called "The Bitter Years," he and his staff pored over some 270,000 photographs in the FSA files. Often without knowing the names of the photographers, they selected 200 photographs for the show. Eighty-five of the pictures chosen had been taken by Lange.

Steichen built on that success to organize one of the most famous photographic exhibition of all time. Beginning in 1954, Lange spent several months helping him. Steichen's brother-in-law, poet and biographer Carl Sandburg, provided a title, "The Family of Man"—a phrase used by Abraham Lincoln.

The Family of Man exhibition, which opened in 1955, contained 503 photographs (including nine of Lange's) by 257 photographers from all over the world. With six traveling exhibits, the show was seen by more than 9 million people in about seventy countries. A book version, also called *The Family of Man* (1955), sold more than 5 million copies and is still in print today.

sea, it left her with a condition called esophagitis, which made it difficult for her to swallow. Radiation was tried and this, too, provided relief, but the improvement was not long-lasting. During periods when she was not laid low by illness, she remained weak and unable to do any serious work.

It was not until 1952 that she felt well enough to try new projects. Her son Dan, after several years living on the streets, had straightened himself out and discovered he had a talent for writing. Together, they prepared an article, illustrated with her photographs, for *Aperture*, a magazine she helped found. They produced another article, about Lange, for *Modern Photography*.

In 1954, Dorothea Lange and Ansel Adams collaborated on a feature story for *Life* magazine about the Mormons, illustrated with thirty-four pictures. *Life* in those years had the largest circulation in the world. The magazine then sent her and Dan to Ireland for another feature. She also spent several months working with Edward

Steichen, helping him prepare his great exhibition and book, *The Family of Man* (1955), which included nine of Lange's pictures. In addition, she taught a few seminars, but these sapped her strength, and she was forced to stop.

Around the World, and Home Again

The United States government asked Taylor to make a trip to Asia in 1958, and he wanted Lange to go with him. She was not eager to face the difficulties of overseas travel, but she did not want to be without him for a stretch of several months. She asked her doctor if she could go. "What does it matter," he replied bluntly, "if you die here or there? Go!"

Between 1958 and 1963, Lange accompanied Taylor on trips to Asia, then South America, and finally the Middle East. In each of the countries, as a representative of U.S. government agencies, he suggested ways to improve the lives of rural populations.

Edward Steichen prepares The Family of Man exhibition.

Lange and her son Dan proved to be an excellent photo-journalism team.

Lange said that the cabin at Steep Ravine "became our special place to be together and to be with the children."

For Taylor's sake, Lange drove herself as hard as her weakened condition would allow. She rode in the backseat of a jeep bouncing over rough roads, ate local foods, which rarely agreed with what she called her "damaged innards," and drank water of questionable purity. On some days, she felt too sick to leave her hotel room and, on several occasions, was rushed to hospitals. She never complained, and Taylor was only occasionally aware of her suffering.

When she could work, Lange went into the fields or crowded city streets with her camera. Although she knew little about the many cultures she encountered, she gradually managed to take some outstanding photographs by focusing on people's faces. In this way, she again found the common human themes of her American photos— love, pain, joy, and sorrow. She also took unusual shots, such as the legs of several children riding on a horse, and close-ups of hands.

During her periods at home, Lange spent more and more time with her family. By the 1950s, all five children were married, and several grandchildren had been born. Lange and Taylor bought a cabin above a rocky cove, naming it "Steep Ravine," and this became the family's favorite gathering place for weekends. The grandchildren felt close to "Grandma Dorie," and they all felt that they gained something special from her presence. They also knew that she was in charge and was never to be opposed.

The family's big Berkeley house was the gathering place for the holidays. From mid-November until New Year's Day, Lange stopped all work to prepare for the great holiday festivities. She bought, or made, presents for the children, spouses, and grandchildren. She spent hours decorating the house and preparing food. The holiday meals lasted several hours, often with more than thirty people at the long table.

From about 1960, the Museum of Modern Art (MOMA) in New York had urged Lange to prepare a one-artist retrospective show. It was a great honor, but she had resisted, partly because she felt that the show would be intensely personal, and she was reluctant to reveal anything about herself.

In the summer of 1964, Lange's health problems changed her mind about the MOMA show. She was feeling weaker than ever, and the pain had moved to her throat. By August, the diagnosis was firm: Lange had cancer of the esophagus. At the time, nearly all patients with this form of cancer died within a year. No surgery was possible; the only treatment was medication to ease the pain. Doctors said she might live only six months or as long as eighteen months.

In all her work, Lange said, she would never "hunt for what was merely 'different'.... If photographers are always looking for the new angle, they miss the world."

CHAPTER SIX

Retrospective

> One should really use the camera as though
> tomorrow you'd be stricken blind. To live a visual
> life is an enormous undertaking, practically
> unattainable. I've only touched it, just touched it.
> —*Dorothea Lange*

From mid-1964 to October 1965, Dorothea Lange spent as much time as she could working on the MOMA exhibit with John Szarkowski, director of the museum's photography department. She was also working on two television documentaries, as well as a photographic essay called "The American Country Woman." Somehow, she managed to find time to spend with her family.

Her husband took care of her physical needs, including serving her breakfast in bed. She could not eat much, only tiny amounts of Jell-O, puddings, and milkshakes. She was growing weaker every day, her weight down to less than ninety pounds. In spite of this, and the constant pain, she managed to work several hours a day on the MOMA exhibit. She never used her camera during that year.

In late summer 1965, Lange cut off social and business contacts, withdrawing more and more into the quiet of home and family. As she had done throughout her illness, she never complained and seemed to have no fear of dying. A friend—the writer chosen to write the introduction to the exhibit catalogue—met with her in June and observed, "She had more true vitality then, despite her pain and imminent death, than most people ever have at any age."

Paul had hoped Dorothea would survive until the opening of the MOMA exhibit in January 1966. In early October, however, she asked to be taken to the hospital, where she died on October 11, 1965. A little earlier in the day she had whispered to Paul, "Isn't it a miracle that this [her final project] comes at the right time!"

Her Legacy

By the 1940s, there were many outstanding photographers in the United States, as well as in Europe. And documentary photography, which was becoming known as photojournalism, remained people's main source of visual images, a dominance that continued until television came of age in the late 1950s.

In this remarkable and important medium, what was there about Dorothea Lange that made her so special? Why, nearly a half-century after her death, do some of her photographs still stand out as adding something new—new to our understanding of our history and to the art of photography? While it may be impossible to describe all the factors that contributed to her greatness, certain qualities stand out.

One key element of her work was her ability to show the human side of huge, seemingly impersonal events, such as the Great Depression or the internment of Japanese Americans. She often achieved this by focusing on an individual. These subjects never seemed posed or even aware of the camera.

In many of her photographs, she added just enough of the background to tell a story. One of her well-known Depression pictures, for example, shows a seated man with his head on his arms, next to him an overturned wheelbarrow. Commenting on this picture, Lange said, "Five years earlier, I would have thought it enough to take a picture of a man, no more. But now, I wanted to take a picture of a man as he stood in his world—in this case, a man with his head down, with his back against the wall, with his livelihood, like the wheelbarrow, overturned."

Another important aspect of Lange's work was her ability to see beyond the pain or suffering caused by events. In her Depression-era photographs, she brought out the courage, stamina, and quiet determination of the American people. These images, as well as the work of a few other outstanding photographers, provide a major reason that the Depression is remembered as one of the heroic episodes in the nation's history.

While Lange's photographs have great artistic power, and often beauty, they may be more important as historical evidence. In writing about the exhibit and the book by Richard and Maisie Conrat, *Executive Order 9066: The Internment of 11,000 Japan-*

Opposite: Lange's photo captured the despair felt by millions of Americans during the Great Depression.

Photo of a sharecropper from Alabama, called "Hoe Culture."

ese Americans, for example, critic A.D. Coleman pointed out "the significant use of the photograph as evidence, not as graphic design or art object. [The photographs] happen to be superbly made pieces of evidence, documents of such a high order that they convey the feelings of the victims as well as the facts of the crime."

The book Lange coauthored with her husband Paul Taylor, *An American Exodus* (1939), extended this concept of photographs as historical evidence to a book combining photos and text. John Szarkowski of MOMA, writing about the 1970 reissue of the book, described it as "one of the best and truest documents we have of the breakdown of America's earlier agrarian ideal. . . . Lange and Taylor demonstrated a new concept of the photographic book, in which the pictures were no longer illustrations, and the text no longer captions, but each maintained its own integrity."

Another of Lange's remarkable array of skills was her ability to focus her camera on a significant gesture. Szarkowski wrote that "she was marvelous with gesture. Not just the gesture of a hand, but the way people planted their feet . . . and held their heads." She often focused her camera on hands, such as in the photograph of an Alabama sharecropper in 1936. The picture shows enough of his torso and his hoe to tell something about him.

When it came to preparing the retrospective exhibit for MOMA, Lange had resisted for several years because she felt it was too personal. She probably agreed to do it when she did—in part at least—because she knew she didn't have long to live.

She approached the show with candid honesty. "In this show," she said, "I would like to be speaking in the sound of my own voice, poor though it may be. Not other people's voices. I would put things in that other people wouldn't. I don't care how wide I lay myself open, this time."

Lange's honest approach to her work, her outstanding photographs, and her contributions to her art and to our understanding of our history combine to make her unique among all American photographers. Critic Nat Herz, writing about the FSA photographers, observed that some of the images had a lasting value because the photographer had produced "something of permanent value that would teach us a little more about man's meaning in this puzzling, often ugly, but deeply beautiful world in which he finds himself." This quality, he concluded, "is very consistently visible in the work of Dorothea Lange. She is not a photographer of the Depression, but an artist for all time."

For Americans in the twenty-first century, it is difficult, perhaps impossible, to understand Dorothea Lange's importance during her lifetime. We are so bombarded by visual images today—in magazines, books, movies, and, above all, television—that

Dorothea Lange described this photo as
"Looking, babe in arms, eyes in the doorway"

we cannot imagine living in the 1920s and 1930s, when the first photo-illustrated magazines appeared. When Lange and a few others began documenting the Great Depression, people had never seen pictures of Dust Bowl conditions or migrant workers making their way into California. When Lange's photo "Migrant Mother" appeared with a news story in newspapers across the country, many Americans were shocked to learn that the people who grew their daily food were themselves starving.

While it's nearly impossible to see Lange's photos in their historical setting, we can still recognize something special about her work: Her deeply felt compassion comes through, often more clearly than in the work of other photographers. At the same time, the person being photographed is frequently looking directly at us across the years. Those images reveal more than pain or sadness, giving us a glimpse of the kind of courage and hope that Americans have displayed throughout history.

GLOSSARY

Auto camps—One-family cabins that motorists rented in pre-motel days (1920–1946).

Bindle stiff—A migrant worker or a hobo who carries his own bedding.

Bohemians—Artists, poets, and writers in San Francisco and New York known for their free and independent lifestyles.

Documentary photography—The use of pictures to provide evidence or to convey a specific message.

Dust Bowl—The region of the Great Plains where overfarming and drought turned topsoil to dust and ruined hundreds of thousands of family farms.

Emulsion—A chemical mixture that forms a coating on a photographic plate, film, or paper.

Farm Security Administration (FSA)—A U.S. government agency. The Historical Division, headed by Roy Stryker, hired some of the nation's greatest photographers to record the impact of the Great Depression on rural America.

Graflex camera—Developed in 1902, a folding camera that produced very sharp pictures and was the standard of professional photographers from the 1920s to the 1950s.

Great Depression—The worst economic downturn in U.S. history, between 1929 and 1940. Government programs of the Franklin Delano Roosevelt Administration provided relief, but full employment did not return until the start of World War II.

Great Plains—An area of grassland that stretches 2,000 miles from southern Canada to southern Texas. Known as "America's breadbasket" because of its extensive grain farms, this entire area was hit hard by the Depression and by the "dust storms" of the 1930s.

Internment—The relocation of 110,000 Japanese Americans to barbed-wire-enclosed camps in remote areas of the country during World War II.

Isei—Japanese immigrants who were born in Japan and were not U.S. citizens.

Nisei—Japanese Americans, born in the United States, who were U.S. citizens.

"Okies"—Nickname for migrant workers who moved to California from Oklahoma and other Dust Bowl states.

Polio—A disease, also known as infantile paralysis, which generally struck children. Frequent epidemics in the first half of the twentieth century took thousands of lives, left thousands more disabled, and spread fear throughout the country until vaccines were developed in the mid-1950s that eliminated the disease in the United States and most of the world.

Prohibition—America's experiment with the outlawing of alcoholic beverages, from 1919 to 1933, which led to widespread violations, including illegal nightclubs (speakeasies) and violence by underworld gangs that controlled the smuggling of alcohol.

Sharecroppers—Farm families who owned no land but farmed on former plantations by giving (sharing) part of their crop to the owner; similar to tenant farming.

Tenant farmers—Farm families who rented cropland, hoping that they could pay the rent with income from selling their harvest. Both tenant farmers and sharecroppers often were victimized by greedy owners who kept them in perpetual debt.

TIME LINE

1895: Dorothea is born on May 26 in Hoboken, New Jersey.

1902: She is stricken with polio, which leaves her partially lame.

1907: Dorothea's father abandons the family; Dorothea takes her mother's maiden name, Lange.

1914: She graduates from high school and starts teacher training. World War I begins (it will end in 1918).

1918: Dorothea Lange heads west, settling in San Francisco.

1919: Lange opens a photographic portrait studio.

1920: She meets and marries Maynard Dixon.

1925: Lange and Dixon have a son, John.

1928: A second son, Daniel, is born to Lange and Dixon. Lange develops her documentary style of photography.

1929: The stock market crashes, and the Great Depression begins (it will last until 1940).

1930: Lange photographs victims of the Depression.

1933: Franklin Delano Roosevelt takes office as president and launches the New Deal to help the American people and revitalize the nation.

1934: Lange tours California, taking photographs with Paul Taylor.

1935: Lange divorces Maynard Dixon and marries Paul Taylor. She is hired by Roy Stryker as a photograpaher for his Department of Agriculture agency.

1936: Lange takes her most famous photograph: "Migrant Mother, Nipomo, California."

1937–1938: A pamphlet with Lange's photos and John Steinbeck's text is published.

1939: Steinbeck's novel *Grapes of Wrath* is published, and a movie based on the book is released. Germany invades Poland, starting World War II (it will end in 1945).

1940: Lange publishes the book *An American Exodus* with Taylor.

1941: Lange is awarded the Guggenheim Fellowship. The Japanese attack the U.S. fleet and military base at Pearl Harbor, Hawaii; the United States enters World War II.

1942: President Roosevelt's Order 9066 requires Japanese relocation. Lange is given the War Relocation Authority (WRA) assignment to photograph the relocation.

1943: Lange photographs the lives of ethnic minorities in San Francisco and in the Richmond shipyards, along with fellow photographer Ansel Adams.

1945: Lange is given the assignment of photographing the United Nations Conference in San Francisco. She becomes seriously ill and has gallbladder surgery.

1952: Lange helps start *Aperture,* a photography magazine.

1954: Lange completes a feature on Mormon life for *Life* magazine. She works with Edward Steichen on an exhibition and book entitled *The Family of Man.*

1958–1963: Lange accompanies her husband, Taylor, on trips around the world.

1964: Lange is diagnosed with inoperable cancer. She works on a retrospective for the Museum of Modern Art (MOMA).

1965: Lange finishes her selections for the MOMA exhibit. She dies on October 11.

FURTHER RESEARCH

ABOUT HER LIFE

Borhan, Pierre, ed. *Dorothea Lange: The Heart & Mind of a Photographer.* Boston: Little, Brown, 2002.

Meltzer, Milton. *Dorothea Lange: A Photographer's Life.* 1978. Syracuse, NY: Syracuse University Press, 2000.

Partridge, Elizabeth. *Restless Spirit: The Life and Work of Dorothea Lange.* New York: Viking/Penguin, 1998.

COLLECTIONS OF PHOTOGRAPHS

Davis, Keith F. *The Photographs of Dorothea Lange.* New York: Harry Abrams, 1995.

Hagen, Charles, ed. *American Photographers of the Depression: Farm Security Administration Photographers, 1935–1942.* New York: Pantheon, 1985.

Lacayo, Richard, and George Russel. *Eyewitness: 150 years of Photojournalism.* New York: Time Books, 1995.

Oakland Museum of California: Dorothea Lange photonegative collection at www.oac.cdlib.org:80/dynaweb/ead/omca.

ABOUT THE PERIOD

King, David C. *American Heritage/American Voices: World Wars and the Modern Age.* Book 4. Hoboken, NJ: Wiley, 2005.

Lingeman, Richard R. *Don't You Know There's A War On? The American Home Front, 1941–1945.* New York: Perigee, 1970.

Starr, Kevin. *Endangered Dreams: The Great Depression in California.* New York: Oxford University Press, 1996.

BIBLIOGRAPHY

Borhan, Pierre, ed. *Dorothea Lange: The Heart & Mind of a Photographer*. Boston: Little, Brown, 2002.

Hagen, Charles, ed. *American Photographers of the Depression: Farm Security Administration Photographs, 1935–1942*. New York: Pantheon, 1985.

Holland, Henry. "Dr. Henry writes about Dorothea Lange." *The Lincolnshire Post-Polio Library:* www.ott.zynet.co.uk/polio/lincolnshire/library/drhenry/dorothealange.

King, David C. *American Heritage/American Voices: World Wars and the Modern Age*. Book 4. Hoboken, NJ: Wiley, 2005.

KQED. "Outtakes from interviews with Dorothea Lange, 1963–1965 for 2 films produced for National Educational Television." Tapes 4-6. San Francisco: KQED, 1965–1966.

Lacayo, Richard, and George Russel. *Eyewitness: 150 Years of Photojournalism*. New York: Time Books, 1995.

Lange, Dorothea. "The Assignment I'll Never Forget: Migrant Mother." *Popular Photography*, February, 1961, 42–43.

Lingeman, Richard R. *Don't You Know There's A War On? The American Home Front 1941–1945*. New York: Perigee, 1970.

Meltzer, Milton. *Dorothea Lange: A Photographer's Life*. 1978. Syracuse, NY: Syracuse University Press, 2000.

Newhall, Nancy. *Ansel Adams: The Eloquent Light*. San Francisco: Sierra Club, 1964.

Oakland Museum of California. Dorothea Lange photonegative collection at www.oac.cdlib.org:80/dynaweb/ead/omca/.

Oliver, Susan. "Profile of Dorothea Lange." www.dorothea-lange.org/Resources/About-Lange.

Partridge, Elizabeth. *Restless Spirit: The Life and Work of Dorothea Lange*. New York: Viking/Penguin, 1998.

Riis, Jacob. *How the Other Half Lives*. 1901. New York: Dover.

Roskin, Mike. "Crown of American Cameras." http://graflex.org/articles/roskin/crown-graphic.html.

Starr, Kevin. *Endangered Dreams: The Great Depression in California*. New York: Oxford University Press, 1996.

Trachtenberg, Alan, and Aperture. *America & Lewis Hine*. Millerton, NY: Aperture, 1977.

INDEX

ABOUT THE AUTHOR

David C. King has written numerous books for young readers, many on American history, such as *The Children's Encyclopedia of American History*, and several biographies, such as *Charles Darwin: A Photographic Story of a Life*. As a sufferer of polio himself, King feels a special connection to Dorothea Lange. He lives with his wife, Sharon, who researches his books, in Hillsdale, New York.

PHOTO CREDITS